THEN & NOW

TOWSON

Melissa Schehlein

To the most supportive, nurturing, and thoughtful friend and mother in the world: this is for you.

To the smartest, sweetest, most loving husband and life partner I could have ever wished for: I share this with you.

Copyright © 2011 by Melissa Schehlein
ISBN 978-0-7385-8734-9

Library of Congress Control Number: 2010936575

Published by Arcadia Publishing
Charleston, South Carolina

Printed in the United States of America

For all general information, please contact Arcadia Publishing:
Telephone 843-853-2070
Fax 843-853-0044
E-mail sales@arcadiapublishing.com
For customer service and orders:
Toll-Free 1-888-313-2665

Visit us on the Internet at www.arcadiapublishing.com

ON THE FRONT COVER: LOOKING NORTHEAST AT THE CORNER OF YORK ROAD AND SUSQUEHANNA AVENUE (NOW TOWSONTOWN BOULEVARD), 1942 AND 2010. This well-travelled crossroads is emblematic of the change that has transformed Towson in the last 75 years. The fondly remembered Ma and Pa (Maryland and Pennsylvania) Railroad regularly meandered its way through the middle of Towson until 1958. The York Road trestle was permanently removed in 1959, and now all that remains are the railroad bridge abutments, seen just right of center in both images. (Then image by Charles Mahan, courtesy of the Baltimore County Public Library (BCPL); Now photograph by the author.)

ON THE BACK COVER: BALTIMORE COUNTY COURTHOUSE, c. WORLD WAR I. Designed in 1854 and completed in 1855, this H-shaped building was enlarged three times between 1910 and 1958. The original cupola was much taller than it now appears, but it proved to be unstable and dramatically swayed in the wind. In 1863, the top two portions of the cupola were removed, leaving the copper-covered dome seen today. (Photograph by C.W.E. Treadwell, courtesy of BCPL.)

THEN & NOW

TOWSON

OPPOSITE: Travelers of a century ago, on their expedition from Baltimore to Pennsylvania, ascended the road to see this view of the center of Towson. Supplies could be purchased at Lee's general store to the left, currency could be exchanged at the Baltimore County Bank on the right, and overnight rest could be found straight ahead at Bosley's Hotel. (Postcard postmarked April 11, 1912, courtesy of James R. Ransom.)

CONTENTS

ACKNOWLEDGMENTS

Jason Domasky, my beloved husband and lifetime companion, longtime webmaster of the Baltimore County Public Library, was invaluable in the creation, execution, and completion of this book. It simply would not have happened without his support, and I am thankful not only for his wise and thoughtful guidance but also his demeanor and sustained positive outlook that raise me up every single day of our lives.

My parents, Kathryn & Rodney Gatzke, provided me with endless pools of support, encouragement, and assistance that helped me maintain my focus and steer this long-worked-on project to fruition. My father, Melvin E. Schehlein, nurtured in me a lifelong passion for computers and technology that inculcated the talent necessary to complete this project. I hope this book makes them just a fraction as proud of me as I am of them.

Richard Parsons amassed a bounty of historic photographs over the past three decades that form the foundation of this book. Dick catalyzed my discovery of countless intriguing stories that elucidate our hometown's past.

John W. McGrain, Baltimore County's paragon of historical knowledge, imparted a bonanza of interesting details that not only filled in the crevices and gaps in my captions but also amplified the veracity and allure of my narrative.

James R. Ransom and John McGrain were generous in allowing me access to their specialized postcard collections that yielded previously undiscovered gems.

Personally, many friends and family facilitated my journey and assisted me along the way. I am very appreciative of their continued friendship and support, and hope I offer the same in return: Rachel Kay, Mario Fernández, Sarah Strasberger, Deidre Anderson, Mary McLaren, Dawn Diffenderfer-Baker, Tina Stenchly-Mohs, Patrice & Felix Morrison, Heidi Buckler, Kirk Bridygham, Karen Possidente-Jean, Ed Baldwin, and Angie Benner.

These photographers generously allowed me to use their images: Dr. William A. Andersen, Spencer Fastie, and Ruth Schaefer. Jim & Thelma Lightner and Jim & Pat Holechek conferred sage advice at a critical stage.

These affable individuals helped me go to high places: Anna Apicella, Bill Hearn, Diane Morris, Don Slaughter, and Lisa Woytek.

The kindness of strangers can sometimes lead you to fun and interesting places. All of the following kind souls thoughtfully assisted me when I asked: Jocelyn Dye, Scott Furman, Sgt. John Kauffman, Brian Keelty, Nancy Hafford, John Manlove, Gerald McHenry, Jack Nye, Charles "Randy" Peaker, Kaitlin Radebaugh, Lisa Radebaugh, Steve Radebaugh, Carol Reidy, Chrissy Saunders, Susan Shea, Steve Walsh, and Sgt. Chris Woodall.

My heartfelt thanks go out to all who assisted me in making this book the best it can be.

All uncredited images were photographed by the author.

REFERENCES

Baltimore County Infobank. www.bcinfobank.com. (Accessed April 2010–September 2010.)

Baltimore County Legacy Web Photograph Collection. www.bcpl.info/legacyweb. (Accessed September 2009–October 2010.)

Baltimore Sun: 1837–1985. Ann Arbor, MI: ProQuest.

Baltimore Sun: 1990–2010. Ann Arbor, MI: ProQuest.

Brooks, Neal A. and Richard Parsons. *Baltimore County Panorama*. Towson, MD: Baltimore County Public Library, 1988.

Brooks, Neal A. and Eric G. Rockel. *A History of Baltimore County*. Towson, MD: Friends of the Towson Library, Inc., 1979.

Diggs, Louis S. *Since the Beginning: African American Communities in Towson*. Baltimore, MD: Uptown Press, 2000.

Furman, Scott. President, Tuxedo House. Interview by author, October 2010.

Gunning, Brooke and Molly O'Donovan. *Towson and the Villages of Ruxton and Lutherville*. Charleston, SC: Arcadia Publishing, 1999.

Hahn, H. George and Carl Behm III. *Towson: A Pictorial History of a Maryland Town*. Norfolk, VA: The Donning Company, 1977.

Keelty, Brian. Historian, Benevolent & Protective Order of Elks, Lodge 469. Interview by author, October 2010.

Lisicky, Michael J. *Hutzler's: Where Baltimore Shops*. Charleston, SC: History Press, 2009.

Maryland Historic Trust's Inventory of Historic Properties. www.mdihp.net. (Accessed April 2010–September 2010.)

McGrain, John W. Retired Baltimore County historian. Interview by author, September 2010.

McHenry, Gerald R. Project Engineer in Water Design Section, Baltimore County Department of Public Works Bureau of Engineering & Construction. Interview by author, October 2010.

Nye, Jack. Director of Facilities Management, Towson University. Interview by author, October 2010.

Parsons, Richard. Author and Researcher/Selector of Baltimore County Legacy Web Photograph Collection. Interview by author, September 2010.

Radebaugh, Kaitlin. Sales Manager, Radebaugh Florist & Greenhouses. Interview by author, October 2010.

Wilson, Hilda N. *Towson Bicentennial 1768–1968 Then . . . Now*. Towson, MD: Junior Press, 1968.

Woodall, Chris. Sergeant in Materials & Facilities Management, Baltimore County Police Department. Interview by author, October 2010.

INTRODUCTION

Towson is the commercial, political, and cultural heart of Baltimore County, Maryland. Historians credit the founding of our fair village to brothers Thomas and William Towson, who settled and farmed at the crossing of York and Joppa Roads. The subsequent subdivision and development of the surrounding land, boosted by the formation of a regionally oriented agricultural and commercial core, nurtured Towsontown through the boom-and-bust economic cycle of 19th- and 20th-century America. The decades following World War II saw an accelerated pace of growth and change as the quaint "town" suffix dropped from common usage. Employers gravitated to the county's high-density hub, attracted by the intermingled spheres of government, law, higher education, and corporate enterprise.

I have endeavored to illustrate the dynamic transformation of the seat of one of the oldest counties in our nation from a centrally located, rural hamlet to the lively, dense urban center it is today. The extensive photograph archive of the Baltimore County Public Library Legacy Web was mined to uncover the gems captured by the photographers of yesteryear, revealing black and white snapshots of York Road, the Baltimore County Courthouse, the Wayside Cross, churches, schools, hospitals, mansions, and well-remembered places that have been sadly lost to the past. Our community has faced relentless growing pains in every modern decade. Towson's built environment and public spaces have been obliterated and transformed so thoroughly that precious few examples remain to tie the present to the distant past.

My primary emphasis is York Road, our defining historical corridor. Many landmarks and vital Towson institutions located along York Road are portrayed. Our gateway landmark, the Solomon Schmuck House, is chronicled as an enduring symbol of an earlier period. The Investment Building, the dramatic first flash of urban growth when it opened in 1960, is recorded in its current state as the widely recognized concrete monolith of Towson, on the cusp of imminent deconstruction to prepare it for conversion to a glass-encased modern edifice. Towson is the hometown of Olympian Michael Phelps, who grew up in Rodgers Forge and graduated from Towson High. His historic accomplishments were recognized this year, along with other local Olympians, by the construction of Olympian Park, which I captured within weeks of its dedication. Hutzler's department store, which presaged the establishment of today's Towson Town Center regional mall, is presented as the forerunner of modern retail in the heart of town. Towson University (formerly Towson State, and before that, the Maryland State Normal College) is depicted in streetscapes that expose Towson's reputation as a college town.

I composed this volume for the enjoyment of longtime residents, newcomers, and native sons and daughters, because the Towson of 90, 60, and 30 years ago was manifestly different from today's landscape of streets, buildings, and houses. Our town and surrounding area is among the most educated in the nation. Towson's high quality of life is affirmed by the desire of locals to remain in the area after retirement. Many of us possess fond memories of the Towson of days gone by, and it is my hope that these pages will serve as a satisfying, vivid essay of the extraordinary changes we experienced during our lifetime.

In these pages, you will observe new buildings appear alongside and behind existing structures, as existing structures grow dense and taller. Trains once traveled through town to the delight of photographers in the past, and these are contrasted with selected views today in which the rail grade, trestle remnants, or all-but-buried rail lines are visible in familiar streetscape settings. Streetcars give way to SUVs, multistory office buildings surround churches, and towers of commerce and industry replace residential houses. Yet in the midst of all this hurried progress, some recognizable footholds of tradition stubbornly refuse to march in step, and these are displayed as a placid reminder that not everything changes.

As I traversed Towson photographing the "now" images, I realized that I was documenting my hometown in a unique period in our nation's history, given the current economic climate. Although our country is not in the throes of an actual depression, to many, it feels like one. It was an eye-opening experience to observe for-sale signs or for-lease banners hanging on every other building in town. Still, progress marches on. I marveled all year long as the Palisades, a new luxury apartment tower, soared floor-by-floor into the skyline until its doors opened to accept new residents. Yet in its shadow, our anachronistic 19th-century jail exhibits a conspicuous for-sale notice. Such is the reality of life in 2010.

Those familiar with Towson may detect the omission of important places that have long since disappeared. As a present-day photographer, I had to rely upon what was shot by my predecessors (who, when known, were credited). This book reflects my comprehensive effort to pair the strongest images of yesteryear with accurate contemporary depictions. I encourage you to indulge and to reminisce.

For additional material that did not fit between these covers, visit my companion website, www.TowsonThenAndNow.com, and feel free to contact me with your comments and feedback.

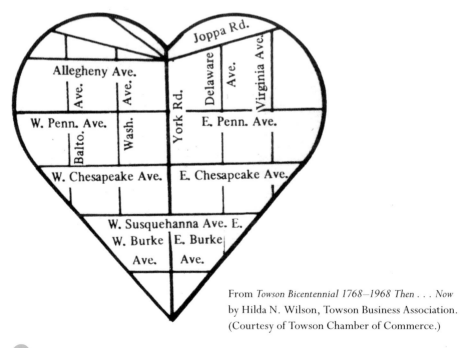

From *Towson Bicentennial 1768–1968 Then . . . Now*
by Hilda N. Wilson, Towson Business Association.
(Courtesy of Towson Chamber of Commerce.)

YORK ROAD
LET'S DRIVE ROUTE 45

TOWSON'S MAIN STREET. A fascinating transformation has occurred along Towson's main artery. This thoughtfully sequenced southbound progression of iconic and everyday streetscape scenes illuminates the changes that have taken place in this important Maryland town within the last 100 years. Above, the Wayside Cross and Towson Hotel are pictured around 1925. The hotel's stone exterior was built sometime in the 1840s and was demolished in 1929. (Courtesy of BCPL.)

LOOKING SOUTH DOWN YORK ROAD NEAR WEST ROAD AT THE BELTWAY, 1909 AND 2002. York Road began as a trail to carry agricultural goods from York, Pennsylvania, to Baltimore. The York Turnpike was established by Baltimore County in 1787 to provide a well-paved toll road, but the project was turned over to a privately owned turnpike company. By the early 1900s, the road had passed to the state of Maryland, and the tolls were eliminated. (Then image by William C. Kenney, courtesy of BCPL; Now photograph by Ruth Schaefer.)

LOOKING SOUTH OVER THE COMMUNITY ORIGINALLY KNOWN AS SANDY BOTTOM, 1951 AND 2010. The Hampton Mansion slave quarters evolved into this African American community of freed slaves in a sandy enclave of this valley. The inhabitants of Sandy Bottom were ultimately forced to relocate in the 1950s and 1960s due to the cost of needed property improvements such as water and sewer lines. Today, businesses thoroughly saturate the area. (Photograph by William Klender, courtesy of BCPL.)

LOOKING SOUTH UP YORK ROAD FROM FAIRMOUNT AVENUE, 1969 AND 2010. Towson's urban fringe has changed little since the summer of the Apollo moon landing. Southbound motorists climbing the 900 block of York Road encounter a jumble of auto-oriented businesses and fast food restaurants. At the top of the hill, one change is evident: the 1932 Towson Water Tower, also known as the Ware Avenue Tank, disappeared from the skyline in 1990. (Courtesy of BCPL.)

MOUNT OLIVE BAPTIST CHURCH, CORNER OF YORK ROAD AND BOSLEY AVENUE, 1977 AND 2010. This historic church is all that remains of the African American pre-emancipation community of Sandy Bottom. Mount Olive, organized in 1888, is associated with Pleasant Rest, a cemetery on high ground overlooking the corner of Bosley Avenue and Kenilworth Drive. Architect Albert Broughton designed the new ark-like building that opened in 1990. (Photograph by Charles Emig, courtesy of BCPL.)

Towson Methodist Episcopal Church in 1913 and Investment Building in 2010. Located at 620 York Road, Towson Methodist Episcopal's 350-seat church was built for $29,000 in 1871. Due to merging Methodist congregations and the growing population in Towson, the church was deconsecrated in 1965 to make way the following year for the 172,500-square-foot, 13-story Investment Building. Prospect Hill Cemetery next door was associated with the church and is the final resting place of many members of familiar Towson families, such as Hillen and Burke. Harris Glenn Milstead, a famous actor more readily known by the name Divine, is also buried there. (Postcard postmarked September 1, 1913, courtesy of James R. Ransom.)

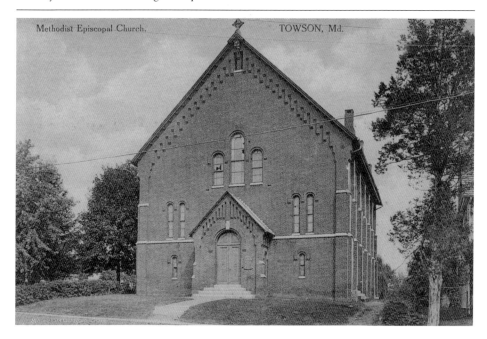

Methodist Episcopal Church.   TOWSON, Md.

SCHMUCK HOUSE AND GINO'S IN 1963 AND M'JOURDELLE IN 2010. Solomon Schmuck's *c.* 1830 Federal-style stone house is thought to be Towson's oldest structure. The property housed generations of successful Towson families before hosting a silversmith, a gun shop, and currently, a bridal boutique. In the 1960s, Baltimore Colts hall-of-famer Gino Marchetti opened one of his many successful hamburger restaurants on the property next door, but now the building serves no apparent purpose and stands as a brown, boarded-up eyesore. (Photograph by Charles Leach, courtesy of BCPL.)

LOOKING EAST ALONG JOPPA ROAD, OVERLOOKING THE INTERSECTION OF YORK ROAD, DULANEY VALLEY ROAD, AND ALLEGHENY AVENUE, 1952 AND 2010. The highest residential density in Baltimore County has been realized along Towson's Joppa Road corridor. Condos and apartment buildings cast long shadows across the offices, restaurants, and parking decks that line the heavily traveled thoroughfare. Hutzler's store entrance below Joppa left a legacy for today's Towson: the street is actually a bridge that was closed for reinforcement in the summer of 2010. (Photograph by the Baltimore County Office of Planning and Zoning, courtesy of BCPL.)

LOOKING SOUTH AT THE INTERSECTION OF YORK ROAD, DULANEY VALLEY ROAD, JOPPA ROAD, AND ALLEGHENY AVENUE, 1967 AND 2010. Perhaps not geographically, but certainly metaphorically, the Towson Circle is the center of town. In the 1960s, this union of four busy arteries crisscrossed at an awkward pair of signaled intersections. The junction was reengineered in 1995 into a high-capacity, oval-shaped traffic roundabout, which decreased traffic delays and fatal accidents as well, making it a safety success. (Photograph by Richmond B. Sullivan, courtesy of BCPL.)

OLYMPIAN PARK, 2006 AND 2010. This pie-slice-shaped property, which festered as a derelict gas station for far too many years, has found new life as an inviting public space that honors the achievement of county residents who have attained Olympic and Paralympic honors. The brand-new park hosts individual monuments recognizing Michael Phelps, Beth Botsford, Katie Hoff, Larry Tyrone Hughes, Jessica Long, and Anita Nall-Richesson. Phelps, who won a mind-blowing eight gold medals in the 2008 Olympics, after earning six gold and two bronze medals in 2004, remains Towson's hometown hero. (Photograph by William A. Andersen.)

Looking North at the 600 Block of York Road, 1965 and 2010. The Investment Building developed a reputation for making some of its tenants' employees sick, and by 2002, it stood virtually empty. In mid-2010, however, the building was given a reprieve, and new developers plan to modernize the building both internally and externally. Once completed, it will be known as Towson City Center. (Photograph by David Turner, courtesy of BCPL.)

YORK ROAD: LET'S DRIVE ROUTE 45

LOOKING WEST ON ALLEGHENY AVENUE FROM YORK ROAD, c. 1910 AND 2010. The bustle of Towson is nowhere more evident than along Allegheny Avenue's healthy commercial corridor. The current site of Towson's weekly farmers market and festivals was once so sleepy that children played games in the street. The tipping point arrived the year of the nation's bicentennial, when construction work on the Penthouse commenced; more than 215 condo units rose into the sky above this economically critical spoke of the roundabout. (Unpostmarked postcard courtesy of James R. Ransom.)

TOWSON FIREHOUSE IN 1910 AND ROUNDABOUT IN 2010. The firehouse was a prominent landmark for nearly a century until it was razed in 1955. It was built by the tenacious Mary Shealy to serve as her general store after two fires in two years destroyed her business. Serving as a community building, at one time or another it housed the armory, a saloon, Catholic mass, a meeting hall, and a band and dance space. It is apropos that it ultimately became the Towson Firehouse until its prime location at this busy junction led to its demise. (Photograph by William C. Kenney, courtesy of BCPL.)

HUTZLER'S BUILDING, 1952 AND 2010. In 1947, Goucher College sold land at the corner of Joppa and Dulaney Valley Roads to Hutzler's department store for the site of the company's first suburban location. Five years later, one month after this construction photograph was taken, it opened for business. As its popularity grew, so did the square footage of the store, with a whole new fourth floor added in 1967. Changing tastes and a series of poor business decisions coincided to inevitably shutter the store completely by the end of the 1980s. (Photograph by Blakeslee-Lane Studio, courtesy of BCPL.)

MEMORIAL DAY OBSERVANCE AT THE WAYSIDE CROSS, 1959 AND 2010. This granite Celtic cross, dedicated in 1921, stands as a memorial to the residents of Baltimore County who gave their lives for their country in World War I. On the four plaques encompassing the base of the monument, 204 names are listed; all are men except for two women, notably listed last. This landmark now serves as the site of periodic celebrations for all veterans, some years with a parade and others with a ceremony. (Photograph by Jack Shipley, courtesy of BCPL.)

Looking South down York Road from the Hutzler's Building, 1975 and 2010. The extended southerly vista enjoyed by pedestrians at the corner of Shealy Avenue exposes the linear character of Towson's main artery. A generation ago, the Little Tavern restaurant served bite-sized burgers across the street from the distinctive Odd Fellows Hall, which has survived the test of time. The Towson Theatre, a single-screen movie house shuttered in 1992, now draws concert visitors and diners as the Recher Theatre and Rec Room. (Photograph by Carl Behm, courtesy of BCPL.)

TOWSON THEATRE, NOW THE RECHER THEATRE, 1965 AND 2010. Costing $100,000 and opening on March 1, 1928, the Towson Theatre was built on the site of the horse stables used by travelers who stayed at the now demolished Towson Hotel (pictured on page 11). The Recher family took possession of the movie palace in 1959, but it took four decades until it transitioned into a live music venue known as the Recher Theatre. (Photograph by David Turner, courtesy of BCPL.)

LOOKING SOUTHWEST ON YORK ROAD TOWARD INTERSECTION WITH PENNSYLVANIA AVENUE, 1920S AND 2010. A popular restaurant once occupied the land upon which the Towson Commons office and retail complex was built in the 1990s. Situated in the shadow of the clock tower atop Lee's corner, Urban's Café was operated by Lewis Urban, the father of Marguerite Urban, who resided for many years in the house next door. Extensive grape arbors were maintained on the property, which later transitioned into the Maryland Restaurant before it closed in the 1960s. (Photograph by William C. Kenney, courtesy of BCPL.)

YORK ROAD: LET'S DRIVE ROUTE 45

LOOKING NORTH AT THE WEST SIDE OF THE 500 BLOCK OF YORK ROAD, 1954 AND 2010. Towson's patriotic pride is in abundance on Independence Day as anticipation mounts for the annual parade. In the summer following the McCarthy hearings, marchers advanced up York Road. Today, spectators line nearby Bosley Avenue while traffic is diverted to Towson's main street. (Courtesy of BCPL.)

NORTHWEST CORNER OF YORK ROAD AND PENNSYLVANIA AVENUE, 1920S AND 2010. The west side of the 500 block of York Road burned, nearly to the ground, in a great fire in January 1878. By 1888, J. Wesley Lee's Store relocated to this two-story building, which stood at the northern end of the new horse-drawn streetcar line. When a streetcar was about to depart for Baltimore City, the clock tower's bell was rung. Five years later, the streetcar line was electrified and overhead live wires were strung. Lee's was the site of Towson's first telephone and was considered an important local institution. (Courtesy of BCPL.)

WEST SIDE OF THE 500 BLOCK OF YORK ROAD, 1963 AND 2010. The Independent Order of Odd Fellows Lodge 79 is the linchpin of the 500 block, casting a timeless shadow across York Road for more than a century and a half. The Yorkhill Lounge, known since the 1970s as the Crease, started in the 1870s as a saloon and restaurant owned by John Maurice Watkins, who fully rebuilt after the 1878 fire. Now the 10-story Towson Commons office building presents a towering backdrop. (Photograph by Charles Leach, courtesy of BCPL.)

LOOKING THROUGH THE SOUTHEAST CORNER OF YORK ROAD AND PENNSYLVANIA AVENUE, 1938 AND 2010. An Esso filling station stood on the site previously used by the Towson Horse Company, a 19th-century livery stable. Towsonians may remember this location as the site of Mano Swartz furriers, who occupied the corner from 1976 until 1992, when the business moved to a less congested location outside of Towson. Hudson Trail Outfitters, who operated here until early 2010, vacated the site soon after the above image was taken. (Photograph by William C. Kenney, courtesy of BCPL.)

32

LOOKING WEST ON CHESAPEAKE AVENUE FROM YORK ROAD, 1972 AND 2010. Parking had become a troublesome issue in Towson by the early 1970s. To accommodate the increasing amount of governmental workers, the county built a new parking facility, shown here. In 1992, the entire block west of York Road between Chesapeake and Pennsylvania Avenues was razed and redeveloped as a retail complex named Towson Commons. Plagued with vacancies, the 384,000-square-foot property, including a 10-story office tower, fell into foreclosure and was sold at auction for $28.5 million in September 2010. (Photograph by David Turner, courtesy of BCPL.)

NORTH SIDE OF EAST CHESAPEAKE AVENUE, c. 1972 AND 2010. More than three dozen years after taxi cabs crowded the unit block of East Chesapeake Avenue, this medley of architecturally clashing facades buzzes with activity on weekdays, with eateries, bail bondsmen, and law offices operating in the shadow of the Towson Library and District Court across the one-way street. (Photograph by David Turner, courtesy of BCPL.)

YORK ROAD: LET'S DRIVE ROUTE 45

LOOKING AT THE SOUTHEAST CORNER OF YORK ROAD AND CHESAPEAKE AVENUE, 1904 AND 2010. A hundred years ago, the intersection of York Road and Chesapeake Avenue was not the bustling junction of today. The horse and buggy ruled the dirt road now prowled by automobiles and Maryland Transit Administration buses. Trees and open vistas greeted the passersby of yesteryear where today the Towson Library's electronic sign proclaims the time and temperature. The library, an example of brutalist architecture designed by the firm of Tatar & Kelly, opened for service on May 13, 1974, after 11 years of planning. (Courtesy of BCPL.)

LOOKING NORTHEAST AT THE CORNER OF YORK ROAD AND SUSQUEHANNA AVENUE (NOW TOWSONTOWN BOULEVARD), 1958 AND 2010. Fifty-odd years ago, the spectacle of freight cars rumbling over the Maryland and Pennsylvania Railroad's York Road overpass was a routine event. Now one can only imagine the vibrations and sound of trains passing through Towson along the telltale grade that parallels the Towson Library. (Photograph by John McGrain, courtesy of BCPL.)

YORK ROAD: LET'S DRIVE ROUTE 45

LOOKING NORTH TOWARD THE 300 BLOCK OF YORK ROAD, 1948 AND 2010. Changing travel and economic patterns affected the fortunes of the Ma and Pa Railroad. Long after reaching its peak just prior to World War I, it halted operations 10 years after the above photograph was taken. By 1960, the York Road trestle was dismantled, leaving the distinctive bridge abutments preserved as evidence of Towson's railroad heritage. Stebbins Anderson, Towson's renowned hardware store, is visible through the overpass at its pre-1980s York Road location; today, the retailer flourishes nearby in the Shops at Kenilworth. (Photograph by John McGrain, courtesy of BCPL.)

LOOKING NORTH AT THE EAST SIDE OF THE 200 BLOCK OF YORK ROAD, 1960S AND 2010. Back when gasoline cost just 29¢ per gallon, this block served the automotive needs of Towsonians. If one wanted an appliance such as an air conditioner or refrigerator, the Towson Economy Store was the place to shop. The Wilson Electric Company, previously located on the block now occupied by Towson Commons and once helmed by fearless Towson promoter Hilda Wilson, changed its name to Wilson Lighting & Interiors when it relocated to the north side of this retail block in the 1990s. (Photograph by David Turner, courtesy of BCPL.)

BOWEN HOUSE, ALSO KNOWN AS THE TUXEDO HOUSE, 40 YORK ROAD, 1977 AND 2010. Built around 1799, this farmhouse, owned by the Bowen family in the 1800s, was a private residence until 1940, when it was reinvented as a Fashion Center for ladies apparel. The stone walls contained one of Towson's biggest open secrets of the decade following World War II: a brothel likely operated above the retail space. From the early 1960s until its razing in 1985, it functioned as the Tuxedo House, still a successful business in nearby Timonium. The Pechter Building occupies the site today. (Photograph by Herbert H. Harwood Jr., courtesy of BCPL.)

LOOKING NORTHEAST AT THE INTERSECTION OF BURKE AVENUE AND YORK ROAD, 1977 AND 2010. A generation of young men was outfitted at this corner in preppy and Ivy League clothing in the conspicuous Oxford Shop, which was long ago transitioned to other uses, such as the M&T Bank branch seen in the above photograph. Traffic routinely overwhelms the capacity of this junction due to its fortuitous position between the central business district and Towson University. (Photograph by the Office of the People's Counsel of Baltimore County, courtesy of BCPL.)

LOOKING WEST AT THE CORNER OF BURKE AVENUE AND YORK ROAD, 1979 AND 2010. The transition from town to gown is nowhere more apparent than at the crossroads of York Road and Burke Avenue. Towson University sprawls south and west of the intersection and the Marriott Conference Hotel, formerly known as the Burkshire, requires all motor and pedestrian traffic to pass below its umbilical campus footbridge. (Photograph by Clement D. Erhardt Jr., courtesy of BCPL.)

LOOKING NORTH ALONG YORK ROAD SHOWING STEPHENS HALL AT TOWSON UNIVERSITY, 1916 AND 2010. The Maryland State Normal College was established with a mission to educate and train public school teachers for the growing state. Once located in the city of Baltimore, the college moved to Towson in 1915 after constructing this Jacobean-style building to house its administrative offices and classrooms. After nearly 100 years and four name changes, the Towson University campus remains under the benevolent watch of Stephens Hall's iconic clock tower. (Photograph by William C. Kenney, courtesy of BCPL.)

ESSO BUILDING, NOW THE TOWSON UNIVERSITY ADMINISTRATION BUILDING, 7720 YORK ROAD, 1958 AND 2010. Esso, later known as Exxon, derived its name from the initials of the Standard Oil corporation, the first tenant of this modernist building. A growth spurt occurred in 1963 with the addition of a floor to each side. The subsequent owner, Citibank, added another floor to the northwest wing in the late 1970s. Because of its location on the perimeter of campus, its availability in 1995 made it an ideal acquisition for the university. (Photograph by Vernon Price, courtesy of BCPL.)

LOOKING NORTH ALONG YORK ROAD AT CEDAR AVENUE, 1917 AND 2010. Today's Cedar Avenue was the original route of York Road in the 18th century. The William Jackson House, just right of center, was built with uncut stone and dates to as early as 1850. It was located next to a large cedar tree, leaving no doubt as to the origin of the street's name. This road to Towson High School, which vehicles can no longer access from York Road, was named Michael Phelps Way in 2004 in recognition of the local Olympian. (Photograph by William C. Kenney, courtesy of BCPL.)

LOOKING SOUTH ALONG YORK ROAD TOWARD STONELEIGH, 1963 AND 2010. In the 1960s, trolleys trundled past Stoneleigh, the neighborhood in southern Towson constructed on the expansive landholdings of Robert P. Brown. The manor house was lost to the mists of time decades ago, but the community retains its distinctive character of mature trees and stately stone and brick single-family homes. (Photograph by Herbert H. Harwood Jr., courtesy of BCPL.)

STEWART'S DEPARTMENT STORE, NOW THE DRUMCASTLE GOVERNMENT CENTER, 6401 YORK ROAD, 1982 AND 2010. The site of the pre–Civil War Drumquhazel mansion has been used as an anchoring commercial area on York Road for half a century. One year after the above photograph was taken, the business was converted into a Caldor discount store. Today, county government offices occupy the renovated building, known by the more easily pronounceable title Drumcastle. (Photograph by Herbert H. Harwood Jr., courtesy of BCPL.)

CHAPTER

COURTHOUSE CORE
TOWSON'S CIVIC HEART

THE COUNTY SEAT. No place in Towson resembles a traditional American village more than the quad of dignified streets that bracket the courthouse complex. The ingredients of the recipe are in abundance: a Keystone Kops police station, a Norman Rockwell post office, a Wall Street bank in miniature, a Gothic church, a Romanesque armory, an imposing cannon, and a menacing jail. This earliest known photograph of the Baltimore County Courthouse, above, dates to around 1865. (Courtesy of BCPL.)

47

BALTIMORE COUNTY POLICE STATION ON WASHINGTON AVENUE, 1939 AND 2010. Originally built as the county police headquarters in 1926–1927, the second floor was added in 1940 for only $869. Two prisoners, a 68-year-old and a 19-year-old veteran, both being detained for minor offenses related to alcohol, perished while sleeping in a cigarette-ignited fire on New Year's Day in 1947. By 1961, growth of the police force required a larger building; Baltimore County Police Department's current headquarters is shown on page 78. The Department of Juvenile Services can now be found in this building. (Courtesy of the Baltimore County Police Department.)

UNITED STATES POST OFFICE
TOWSON, MD.

TOWSON POST OFFICE, SOUTHWEST CORNER OF CHESAPEAKE AND WASHINGTON AVENUES, 1941 AND 2010. When the Towson branch opened in 1938, the cost of the most essential distance-communication tool, a first-class stamp, was only 3¢. In the wake of the Great Depression, Pres. Franklin Roosevelt's New Deal created the Works Progress Administration, which commissioned a tetraptych wall mural on the development of mail transportation that can still be enjoyed in the lobby of this limestone building. (Postcard postmarked August 6, 1941, courtesy of James R. Ransom.)

MARYLAND NATIONAL GUARD ARMORY (TOWSON ACADEMY), 1963 AND 2010. Towson will be well protected in the event of an emergency by two National Guard armories: the Ruhl armory at the York Road Beltway junction and this centrally located Washington Avenue armory. The structure resembles a medieval fortification and was built in 1933 for $75,000 on the site of the well-established Smedley House Hotel after it burned to the ground, killing a cook in the process. The armory is the headquarters of Charlie Company and also serves as a congenial gathering place for dance lessons and county employee receptions. (Photograph by Charles Leach, courtesy of BCPL.)

COURTHOUSE CORE: TOWSON'S CIVIC HEART

NORTHWEST CORNER OF WASHINGTON AND CHESAPEAKE AVENUES, 1950S AND 2010. The No. 8 Line once traced an arc through this junction, delivering passengers who had business with the county government or its nearby institutions. Decades of paving and milling converted the intersection into a palimpsest of Towson's streetcar past: the curved rails can still be seen embedded in the asphalt, but disappeared soon after the above photograph was taken due to the commencement of a streetscape beautification project that began along Washington Avenue. (Photograph by Herbert H. Harwood Jr., courtesy of BCPL.)

LOOKING NORTHEAST FROM COURTHOUSE PARK TOWARD WASHINGTON AVENUE, 1956 AND 2010. This bronze cannon, cast in Seville in 1781, was captured from the Spanish arsenal during the 1898 Battle of Manila Bay during the Spanish-American War. On the fifth anniversary of the war, the cannon was placed on a granite pedestal in front of the courthouse. The cannonballs accompanying this war relic were welded together in the late 1930s to prevent children from rolling the balls onto the nearby trolley car tracks. (Photograph by John McGrain.)

COURTHOUSE CORE: TOWSON'S CIVIC HEART

East Side of 400 Block of Washington Avenue on Fourth of July 1954 and Towsontown Spring Festival 2010. A modest row of buildings once fronted Washington Avenue, festooned in the summer of 1954 with pennants and bunting. Banks constructed the bookended pair of multistory office buildings that overlook festival crowds every spring. This section of the road was closed for an extended period in 2010 due to the Washington Avenue streetscape project. (Courtesy of BCPL.)

LOOKING EAST ALONG PENNSYLVANIA AVENUE AT WASHINGTON AVENUE FROM THE NORTHEAST SIDE OF THE OLD COURTHOUSE, 1958 AND 2010. In 1868, Thomas Todd constructed the tiny building seen at the end of the iron fence to serve as an office for the law firm of Gittings, Machen, and McIntosh. Since the days that streetcars rolled along Washington Avenue, the growth of office buildings surrounding the courthouse is evident, as seen through the blanket of snow laid by the twin blizzards of 2010. (Courtesy of BCPL.)

COURTHOUSE CORE: TOWSON'S CIVIC HEART

COLONEL MCINTOSH'S LAW OFFICE IN 1969 AND YMCA TOWSON FAMILY CENTER IN 2010. David Gregg McIntosh was a lawyer before the Civil War, served as a Confederate artillery soldier during the war, and finally settled in this little brick building in Towson to work in his chosen profession. In 1969, in order to preserve the historic structure, it was moved from its location across from the courthouse to the grounds of the Towson YMCA, formerly the Kelso Home for Girls. Built in 1925 as an orphanage, the large building at top right is slated for demolition and replacement. (Courtesy of BCPL.)

NORTHEAST CORNER OF BALTIMORE COUNTY COURTHOUSE, 1934 AND 2010. Since the days of the Great Depression, the courthouse complex has attracted automotive and pedestrian traffic. As recently as 25 years ago, the land surrounding the structure was bereft of manicured gardens and ornamental plantings. In the late 1980s, renowned landscape architect and Towson resident Wolfgang Oehme shaped the grounds visitors enjoy today. Visitors and governmental workers seeking a quick lunch on the run can make a pilgrimage to the hot dog cart of Dan Demopulos. (Photograph by Jeanette Hilgartner, courtesy of BCPL.)

LOOKING NORTHEAST AT THE 100 BLOCK OF WEST PENNSYLVANIA AVENUE AND CALVARY BAPTIST CHURCH, 1963 AND 2010. The Calvary Church was formed in the 1890s. During the erection of a new church building in 1929, the 1892 wood sanctuary, which had been moved off the original foundation, was destroyed by fire. Construction continued as planned, and the existing Gothic building was completed with locally quarried quartzite stone. In the meantime, the congregation held services in the Towson Theatre. (Photograph by Charles Leach, courtesy of BCPL.)

ORIGINAL BALTIMORE COUNTY JAIL, BOSLEY AVENUE AND TOWSONTOWN BOULEVARD, 1926 AND 2010. The gallows that once stood adjacent to the 1854 Towson jail represented the severity of criminal justice during the 19th century and well into the 20th century. This lethal punishment was most often meted out to the poorest citizens with the darkest skin tones. These public events typically occurred at daybreak, creating a ghoulish near-party atmosphere in the surrounding streets the overnight before. (Postcard postmarked November 5, 1926, courtesy of John McGrain.)

COURTHOUSE CORE: TOWSON'S CIVIC HEART

FAMILIAR LOCAL SCENES. The whole is greater than the sum of its parts, but the individual parts paint the brightest portrait. Parks, plazas, rail stations, schools, shops, malls, manor houses, hospitals, houses of worship, and high-rises blend like the pigments on an artist's palette to form the vibrant colors of everyday life in Towson. The *Towson News* was published from June 1905 to August 1909. (Postcard postmarked October 15, 1906, courtesy of James R. Ransom.)

BEST PRODUCTS COMPANY SHOWROOM IN 1978 AND TARGET IN 2010. Eudowood Plaza in the 1980s hosted this attention-grabbing building facing Goucher Boulevard. The "Tilt Showroom" boasted a 450-ton masonry-block facade resting at a 35-degree angle. BEST Products president Andrew Lewis, below right, is shown at its opening in 1978 with architect James Wines, who hailed from the area and is a graduate of Towson High School, class of 1950. Ultimately, the catalog retailer went out of business, and the building was razed in 1997. (Courtesy of BCPL.)

LUSKIN'S, 1971 AND 2010. Jack Luskin, who became a local celebrity as "the cheapest guy in town," founded the popular electronics store in 1948. The Towson location sat on the crest of a ridge that became known as Luskin's Hill, which overlooks Interstate 695 at Cromwell Bridge Road. Many Towsonians remember Luskin's fondly due to their annual Fourth of July fireworks display. Fit! Gym now occupies the location. (Photograph by Vernon Price, courtesy of BCPL.)

Trinity P. E. Church, Towson, Md.

TRINITY (PROTESTANT) EPISCOPAL CHURCH, 120 ALLEGHENY AVENUE, 1909 AND 2010. The Trinity congregation worships in the oldest church in Towson, built in 1860 with a nave designed by Norris Starkweather. John Ridgely of Hampton donated the limestone used in the construction of the Romanesque exterior. Since 1971, the Surprise Shop, a volunteer-staffed thrift enterprise, has operated in Trinity's old rectory. (Postcard postmarked April 13, 1909, courtesy of James R. Ransom.)

CHURCH OF THE IMMACULATE CONCEPTION, 200 WARE AVENUE, 1940S AND 2010. The striking church high up on the ridge is a venerated icon of Towson, with its origins steeped in the history of the rising Catholic population in the area. Around 1900, the distinctive Christian monogram "IHS" was worked into the new slate roof in recognition of airplane traffic passing overhead. Immaculate Conception operated a nearby private high school named Towson Catholic for 86 years until it closed in 2009. (Unpostmarked postcard courtesy of John McGrain.)

Kraushaar Auditorium and Dorsey College Center, Goucher College, 1964 and 2010. Dr. Otto Kraushaar was the campus president who shepherded the college's transition from its small Baltimore city location to the expansive Towson campus. Rhoda Dorsey, a history professor, became the first female president of the college, and the admission of male students occurred during her tenure. The 995-seat auditorium and the administrative building were named after them to honor their contributions to Goucher. (Photograph by Herbert H. Harwood Jr., courtesy of BCPL.)

Auburn House, Towson University, 1973 and 2010. The widowed Rebecca Ridgely was the first resident of Auburn House, built in 1790 as a smaller version of Hampton Mansion. The residence was named for "Sweet Auburn" in Oliver Goldsmith's 1770 poem *The Deserted Village*. A lightning strike caused the house to burn to the ground in 1849, but it was subsequently rebuilt in the Greek Revival style. After falling into disrepair and being mercilessly vandalized in the early 1970s, it was acquired and completely renovated by Towson State University. (Photograph by Kenneth T. Wright Sr., courtesy of BCPL.)

RIDERWOOD RAILROAD STATION, 1972 AND 2010. Located just north of Joppa Road on the outskirts of Ruxton, this station was built by the Northern Central Railroad (NCRR) in 1905, after the original waiting shed burned down. After the last train stopped there in 1959, the station became the home of a longtime NCRR employee and his family, who lived there for 40 years. The rails, now protected by a fence, are used by the Maryland Transit Administration's light rail system. (Photograph by Kenneth T. Wright Sr., courtesy of BCPL.)

TOWSON: IN GENERAL

TOWSON ESTATES' 14TH-CENTURY ITALIAN MARBLE WELL, 1920s AND 2010. Walter Mylander developed Towson Estates, advertised as the "Ideal Suburb," to cater to Black & Decker and Bendix executives and their families with stately stone rental homes. He imported this ancient Italian well and installed it on a framework of stone quarried in Butler, Maryland. Situated off Joppa Road and now well hidden by walls of vegetation, only the foundation remains, as the well itself was removed long ago. Other fountains, however, can be found nestled within the community. (Courtesy of BCPL.)

BOSLEY MANSION, NOW PRESBYTERIAN HOME OF MARYLAND, 1972 AND 2010. Grafton M. Bosley, a physician, held significant Towson-area landholdings in the 1850s. He donated the land for the Odd Fellows Hall on York Road, and he granted 5 acres for the county courthouse and jail. Bosley, who foresaw the looming Civil War, built this mansion in West Towson as his home in 1856 with a cupola that served as a lookout for signs of the impending armed conflict. In 1929, it became the Presbyterian Home of Maryland, which now serves as an assisted living facility for seniors. The resident canine, a golden retriever, is named Bosley. (Photograph by Kenneth T. Wright Sr., courtesy of BCPL.)

OLD TOWSON LIBRARY, 1963 AND 2010. Prior to 1974, the Towson branch and administrative offices of the Baltimore County Public Library occupied this building on West Susquehanna Avenue near the southern edge of the courthouse core. Growth and increased demand for services required a new building to be constructed a few blocks to the east. The Health Concern, a natural foods store, currently operates within the modest brick structure. (Photograph by Charles Leach, courtesy of BCPL.)

DUMBARTON MANSION, 1910 AND 2010. Built in 1853 on land originally owned by philanthropist Johns Hopkins, this Greek Revival–style mansion sat on a large estate formerly named Friends Discovery, which was later subdivided to become the community of Rodgers Forge. Dumbarton Middle School surrounds the manor house on three sides, obstructing its visibility from Dumbarton Road. It currently serves as the home of the Baltimore Actors' Theatre Conservatory. (Courtesy of BCPL.)

VILLA ANNESLIE, 529 DUNKIRK ROAD, 1857 AND 2010. Frederick Harrison, a civil engineer who surveyed railroads, built this romantic Italianate two-story villa on a working farm as his summer home. He named it for his daughter Anne, who married Lennox Birckhead, whose family passed on the home to many generations. In the 1920s, the acreage around the villa was sold and subdivided to form the Anneslie neighborhood. (Drawing from Robert Taylor's 1857 map, courtesy of BCPL.)

RADEBAUGH FLORIST & GREENHOUSES, 120 EAST BURKE AVENUE, C. 1942 AND 2007. George Radebaugh and his wife, Anna, shown in the vintage image below, started their flower-growing business in 1924. Florists suffered during the Great Depression, briefly spurring the entrepreneurial family into the pond and pool installation business. After moving to the current site between Central and Maryland Avenues in 1940, George and Anna raised five children on the property while living above the store. Today, the third and fourth generations of Radebaughs manage the family-owned enterprise, including (clockwise from left in the above image) Ned, Doug, Steve, Sean, Derek, Joe, Jesse, and the greenhouse pups, Abby and Bailey. (Then image courtesy of Lisa Radebaugh; Now photograph by Spencer Fastie.)

BLACK & DECKER WORLD HEADQUARTERS, 621 EAST JOPPA ROAD, C. 1970 AND 2010. In 1910, S. Duncan Black and Alonzo G. Decker started a machine shop business in Baltimore. After obtaining the world's first patent for a portable power tool, they chose Towson as the location of their first factory. By the early 1940s, Black & Decker began war manufacturing for the Allies. When war production declined, they shifted their focus to tools for hobbyists; business boomed. In early 2010, Black & Decker merged with Stanley Works. The expansive Stanley Black & Decker complex is Towson's inescapable east-side superblock, compelling residents and commuters to circumnavigate the secure premises on a sinuous course of intersecting streets. (Photograph by W.R. Atkinson, courtesy of BCPL.)

Looking West over the Downtown of Towson from the TABCO Building on Joppa Road, 1987 and 2010. In this elevated panoramic view over the 500 block, the subtle evolution of Towson is revealed. Towson Burger King, or TBK as it was affectionately known by a generation of local teenagers, is shown in the center of the above image surrounded by cars. Less than 25 years later, the restaurant relocated to the 900 block of York Road, and the shuttered and fire-damaged property awaits redevelopment on the site of the proposed Towson Circle III project, which has suffered delays.

LOOKING NORTHWEST OVER THE TOWSON TOWN CENTER MALL FROM THE TABCO BUILDING, 1987 AND 2010. Built on land sold by Goucher College from a parcel of the original Hampton Estate, Towson Plaza started as a two-level, open-air strip shopping center in 1959. After three major renovations that incorporated the Hecht's building and Hutzler's parking lot, the Towson Town Center now stands as an imposing four-level, first-class shopping destination.

TOWSON PLAZA SHOPPING CENTER, NOW TOWSON TOWN CENTER, 1970 AND 2010. While seeking the presidency in September 1960, Senator John F. Kennedy selected the recently opened Towson Plaza as the Baltimore location to give a campaign speech. The *Baltimore Sun* reported that approximately 3,500 people were on-hand to support the charismatic Kennedy, who announced that his "New Frontier offers the opportunity for all people to be of service to the nation in the years ahead." (Photograph by David Turner, courtesy of BCPL.)

HAMPTON PLAZA AND HAMPTON HOUSE APARTMENTS, 1972 AND 2010. Built as a luxury high-rise to meet the growing housing demand in Baltimore County, Hampton House's 14 floors and 199 apartments opened in 1965. Six years later, Hampton Plaza opened with its dual semicircular towers—one for apartments and one for offices. The complementary buildings, although now displaying different exterior colors, are situated on East Joppa Road and overlook the sprawling Towson Town Center. Hampton House has been renamed the Berkshires at Town Center. (Photograph by Kenneth T. Wright Sr., courtesy of BCPL.)

MARYLAND BLUE CROSS AND BLUE SHIELD BUILDING, NOW THE BALTIMORE COUNTY PUBLIC SAFETY BUILDING, 700 EAST JOPPA ROAD, 1972 AND 2010. Now serving as headquarters of the county's police and fire departments, this mirrored-glass-clad structure was cleverly designed with the entrance and parking lot hidden underneath the building's surrounding grassy knolls. Respected Baltimore architects Peterson & Brickbauer designed this curtain-wall-style building with a smaller, contrasting mechanical housing cube covered in bright red glazed brick. To the author's family, it was always known as "the Flashcube." (Courtesy of BCPL.)

LOOKING EAST AT THE CORNER OF BOSLEY AND ALLEGHENY AVENUES, 1976 AND 2010. Bosley Avenue was rerouted and widened in the 1970s to form a segment of the Towson Bypass, created to divert traffic around York Road's most congested section. Most Towsonites regard this dimidiate thoroughfare as the dividing line between the leafy neighborhoods of West Towson and the hyper-development of the central business district. The Penthouse, a Peter Christie–designed building that was known for a brief time as Towson Towers, looms large in the landscape. (Photograph by Kenneth T. Wright Sr., courtesy of BCPL.)

ST. JAMES AFRICAN UNION METHODIST PROTESTANT CHURCH, 415 JEFFERSON AVENUE, 1976 AND 2010. The bell that once rested on the roof pedestal of this 19th-century house of worship proved to be too heavy for the building. Today, the device is displayed in an enclosure on the grounds of the oldest African American congregation in Towson, founded in 1861. At one time, this was the bell in the tower at Lee's corner (seen on page 30) that rang to announce the departure of a streetcar bound for Baltimore City. (Photograph by Carl Behm, courtesy of BCPL.)

Looking North on Hillen Avenue in East Towson, 1980 and 2010. Hampton Mansion owner Gov. Charles Carnan Ridgely freed most of his slaves upon his death in 1829. Many settled not far from the mansion, purchasing land and building homes, contributing to the stability and endurance of this East Towson community. Mount Calvary African Methodist Episcopal Church sits on the land once occupied by a row of modest homes facing Hillen Avenue near its distinctive bend. (Photograph by Herbert H. Harwood Jr., courtesy of BCPL.)

DANIEL LEE HOUSE, 100 EAST PENNSYLVANIA AVENUE, 1974 AND 2010. Built around 1876, this 12-room stone structure at the southeast corner of Delaware and Pennsylvania Avenues was part of the sizable Daniel Lee estate in East Towson. Though it is unclear if Daniel actually lived in the house, it is considered to be one of Towson's oldest structures. The building was thoroughly renovated in the 1980s and is currently occupied by the family dentistry practice of J. Karl Sachs. (Photograph by Kenneth T. Wright Sr., courtesy of BCPL.)

ELKS LODGE NO. 469, 4 WEST PENNSYLVANIA AVENUE, FOURTH OF JULY 1910 AND THE 2010 TOWSONTOWN SPRING FESTIVAL. A stained-glass Palladian window welcomes members to the Benevolent & Protective Order of Elks, which formed their charter in 1899. Built in 1905, this is the oldest Elks lodge in the country specifically designed for and continually used by the Elks, having never served as a private residence. The first and second floors have an open layout to accommodate the meeting needs of its membership, and a large wooden bar welcomes all who enter. (Photograph by William C. Kenney, courtesy of BCPL.)

AIGBURTH VALE, 1950 AND 2010. Comedian John E. Owens (1824–1886) purchased nearly 200 acres of Rock Spring Farm and built this costly mansion in 1868, naming it Aigburth Vale, probably because he was born in the Aigburth area of Liverpool, England. Located at 212 Aigburth Road, the country home of the popular humorist is an example of Second Empire architecture. It now serves as an independent senior apartment community, sharing its front yard with the grounds of Towson High School. (Photograph by John McGrain.)

THE RIDGE MANSION, 1977 AND 2010. Located at 1306 West Joppa Road, this 30-room mansion was built in 1898 by George W. Abell, son of the founder of the *Baltimore Sun* newspaper. For the latter half of the 20th century, the yellow-brick structure was used as the Ridge School, serving special education students until 2000. Now, it is once again a private residence. (Photograph by Herbert H. Harwood Jr., courtesy of BCPL.)

LOYOLA BLAKEFIELD, 1971 AND 2010. Loyola High School was established in 1852 in Baltimore City but moved to Towson in the late 1930s as a result of the support provided by the Blake family. When the sixth, seventh, and eighth grades were added, this private Catholic school changed its name to Loyola Blakefield. Arguably the school's most famous alumnus is Tom Clancy, whose most well-known fictional character, Jack Ryan, is also a Loyola graduate. (Photograph by Kenneth T. Wright Sr., courtesy of BCPL.)

St. Joseph Hospital and Medical Center, 7601 Osler Drive, 1970s and 2010. St. Joseph's humble beginnings can be traced to 1864, when three houses on North Caroline Street in Baltimore City were given to the Sisters of St. Francis in order to care for the sick and infirm, as patients were termed back then. In 1867, a hospital was built downtown; by 1965, demand necessitated a larger facility, a site in Towson was selected, and the award-winning medical center was constructed for a reported cost of $11 million. (Courtesy of BCPL.)

SHEPPARD AND ENOCH PRATT HOSPITAL'S CHARLES STREET GATEHOUSE, 1977 AND 2010. Caring for the mentally ill with "courteous treatment and comfort" was an innovative concept more than a century ago, but Moses Sheppard (1771–1857) proved he was well ahead of his time. Despite what the original, now-antiquated name of Sheppard Asylum may have implied, Sheppard's stipulated mission was "curative, combining science and experience for the best possible results." In 1860, this gatehouse designed by John Gettier was the first building constructed on campus. Throughout the 20th century, vehicles could drive through the structure, but after too many trucks became lodged in the archway, traffic was routed around it. (Photograph by G.W. Fielding, courtesy of BCPL.)

SHEPPARD AND ENOCH PRATT HOSPITAL'S B BUILDING, EARLY 1900S AND 2010. Sheppard's mission was augmented by an endowment from Enoch Pratt (1808–1896) at the time of his death. Taking nearly 30 years to complete, the Calvert Vaux–designed A and B buildings are mirror images of each other, with one intended to house men and the other women. In the early 1970s, the Central building, on the right in the photograph below, bridged the original 100-foot-wide space between A and B. (Photograph by Jacques Kelly, courtesy of BCPL.)

TOWSON HIGH SCHOOL (1907–1925) ON ALLEGHENY AVENUE, 1907 AND 2010. East Chesapeake Avenue was the site of the original Towson High School building, which succumbed to fire in 1906; this Smith & May–designed 1907 building was its replacement. Starting with an enrollment of 90 at dedication, the L-shaped building housed all grades. When the student population quadrupled, a new school was erected just behind it, and the facility many Towsonians call the "Old Towson High School" became a grammar school. It now houses Baltimore County government offices. (Postcard postmarked May 6, 1907, courtesy of James R. Ransom.)

TOWSON HIGH SCHOOL (1925–1949) ON CENTRAL AVENUE, 1927 AND 2010. This second Smith & May building may now serve the needs of seniors as the BYKOTA Center (Be Ye Kind, One To Another), but its original purpose was to shape growing minds. By the early 1930s, Towson's growing population made the addition of the third floor a necessity. Ultimately, it followed the same path as the building before it—when a newer high school opened, it became an elementary school. (Postcard postmarked October 11, 1927, courtesy of James R. Ransom.)

TOWSON HIGH SCHOOL (1949–PRESENT), CEDAR AVENUE ENTRANCE, 1976 AND 2010. For the last 60 years, Towson's youth have passed through the halls of this structure, including the author of this book (class of 1988). The stone building underwent two major changes, the first in the 1960s for the science and library wing addition and the second in the 1990s that included air-conditioning. For the students, the *Talisman* reports the news; *Sidelights* presents the faces. (Photograph by Carl Behm, courtesy BCPL.)

TOWSON HIGH SCHOOL (1949–PRESENT), AIGBURTH AVENUE ENTRANCE, 1976 AND 2010. Nathan Towson was the 12th child of Towson's first businessman, Ezekiel Towson, and grandson of one of the town's founders, William Towson. Nathan was called to defend the country in the War of 1812; after showing several acts of gallantry, he rose to the rank of major general. This is the reason many generations of teenagers from the area have memories of being a General. (Photograph by Paul Dorsey, courtesy of BCPL.)

LOCH RAVEN DAM, 1971 AND 2010. Although technically not located within Towson's traditional borders, the Loch Raven Reservoir has provided nearly a century of outdoor recreation to its surrounding residents. The lower dam, not shown, dates from the 1870s, but this upper dam was built in two phases in 1914 and 1922. It permits the collection of 23 billion gallons of fresh water and supplies the majority of Baltimore's drinking water. In 2005, the face of Loch Raven Dam was completely rehabilitated and resurfaced, securing its safety and reliability for generations to come. (Photograph by Kenneth T. Wright Sr., courtesy of BCPL.)

INDEX

www.arcadiapublishing.com

Discover books about the town where you grew up, the cities where your friends and families live, the town where your parents met, or even that retirement spot you've been dreaming about. Our Web site provides history lovers with exclusive deals, advanced notification about new titles, e-mail alerts of author events, and much more.

Arcadia Publishing, the leading local history publisher in the United States, is committed to making history accessible and meaningful through publishing books that celebrate and preserve the heritage of America's people and places. Consistent with our mission to preserve history on a local level, this book was printed in South Carolina on American-made paper and manufactured entirely in the United States.

Find Your Place in History.